Teachings That Must Not Be Lost
Volume I

Grace

The Power of God and the Promise of the New Covenant

Paul F. Pavao

Copyright 2015. Paul F. Pavao. All rights reserved.

Notes

1. Unless otherwise noted, all Scripture references are based on the King James Version, then updated and punctuated to conform with modern American English.

2. Because "Christ" has, for the most part, lost its meaning in modern Christianity, being reduced to a name rather than a title, I have replaced it, in most cases, with an actual translation: "King." See http://www.paulfpavao.com/christos-transliteration.html for a longer explanation of why I do this.

Introduction

I gave my life to King Jesus in 1982. In those early days I attended an Assembly of God church and visited a couple other Protestant denominations. Having been raised Catholic, I was very excited about my new life in a church for which the Bible was "the sole rule of faith and practice."

It didn't take me long to find out that Protestants have grave disagreements about what that "sole rule" is. Every denomination interpreted the Bible differently, argued with other denominations about it, and no one changed their minds.

More than thirty years have passed, and Protestant churches don't emphasize doctrine as much as they used to. They still meet separately as Assembly of God, Baptist, Presbyterian, Methodist, and many other denominations, but now quite a lot are "non-denominational."

My concern is not so much theological as it is practical. Paul was confident of his churches that each member would continue to grow in Jesus throughout their lives because "he who began a good work in you will complete it until the day of King Jesus" (Php. 1:6). Looking around as a young Christian, that is not what I saw. I saw that maybe 10% of the Christians in the churches I attended were growing in Jesus. Most were growing less and less interested in the Christian faith and getting more and more caught up in other interests.

George Barna is the leading Christian pollster of our time, and his polls say that in this matter, things haven't changed much:

Although people cite their primary reasons for attending church as growing closer to God and learning more about him, Barna Group finds such closeness is a rare occurrence. Fewer than two out of ten churchgoers feel close to God on even a monthly basis. Additionally, while almost two-thirds of those who value church attendance go to learn more about God, fewer than one in ten (6%) who have ever been to church say they learned something about God or Jesus the last time they attended. In fact, the majority of people (61%) say they did not gain any significant or new insights regarding faith when they last attended.[1]

I don't think the problem is the disinterest of Americans in the claims of King Jesus. I think Protestant churches have so misrepresented the claims of King Jesus that the people in them have little idea of what it means to be a Christian.

This series of booklets is meant to show you what it means to be a Christian and to get you properly founded in the teaching of the apostles as found in the Scriptures and in the churches that they formed 2,000 years ago.

---

[1] https://www.barna.org/barna-update/culture/661-americans-divided-on-the-importance-of-church#.VUEetBcmAiG, accessed Apr. 29, 2015

Grace: The Favor of God

Grace, in every practical sense in Scripture, is divine power. Despite the fact that the word is rarely used that way by Christians, the Scriptures demonstrating this usage are clear, common, and consistent.

The definition of grace, *charis* in Greek, is generally given as "favor" or "unmerited favor" in lexicons, though "unmerited" is a doctrinal addition, not anything actually implied by *charis*.

A good way to understand this definition is to consider the favor of an earthly ruler. For example, I knew a lady whose uncle was the military dictator of a small country. The dictator's favor would have guaranteed her a luxurious lifestyle back in her country.

Oddly enough, she was not living in her country. Instead, she was living in relative poverty in a European country. When I asked her why, she said that if she partook in the luxuries of her uncle's reign, she would also partake in the punishments when his dictatorship was overthrown, as it surely would be.

My friend got no benefits from the favor of her dictator uncle. To have the favor of God, however, provides benefits that will not be regretted because God will never be overthrown. To have the favor of God provides benefits that no earthly ruler could provide, because God's rule is over everything and lasts forever.

Scripture often discusses how to obtain the favor of God, but as we can see from my friend's uncle, favor that is not used may as well have not been obtained.

Let me say that again. Favor that is not used may as well have never been obtained.

Scripture talks about how to *obtain* the favor of God and, just as importantly, it discusses how to *use* it. Because, however, the source of the grace of God (apart from works) was such a hot topic during the Reformation, Protestants tend to focus only on how to obtain God's favor rather than on how to use it. In other words, because we are so focused on the fact that God's grace is a free gift, we forget to find out what benefits we have obtained from that favor!

God's Riches At Christ's Expense

GRACE:

> **G**od's
> **R**iches
> **A**t
> **C**hrist's
> **E**xpense

I love this acronym. How unfortunate that because we focus so much on "Christ's Expense," we often forget to partake of "God's Riches."

This fault is so common and so deep that most evangelicals have no idea that they are missing out on anything, much less the details of what they are missing out on.

In Ephesians 1 Paul prays for the saints that we would know three exceptional, extraordinary, abundant things:

1. The hope of our calling (v. 18; cf. Php. 3:13-14)
2. The "riches" of the glory of his inheritance in the saints (v. 18)
3. The "surpassing greatness" of his power towards us who believe, the very same power that raised Jesus from the dead (v. 19)

We evangelicals love to talk about the hope of our calling. We talk some about the riches of the glory of God's inheritance in the saints. We may even talk about the surpassing greatness of his power if we teach about spiritual gifts and miracles.

I submit to you, however, that the "surpassing greatness of his power" is summed up in the word "grace." At Jesus' expense, we have entered into the favor of God, and God's favor—grace—brings us the benefits of a power so great that it raised Jesus from the dead and will raise us all up as well.

We don't have to wait until the resurrection to experience that power. We have already entered the favor of God, every bit as much as Jesus did because Jesus purchased that favor for us.

Grace and Mercy

Oddly enough, evangelicals[2] consistently use the word "grace" in a way that has nothing to do with how to obtain it or walk in its benefits. Instead, it is used primarily as a synonym for mercy. For example, if someone wrongs me, an evangelical might encourage me to "show that person grace." What the evangelical is trying to tell me is that I should forgive the person who wronged me and forget the wrong done to me.

Grace, however, is the wrong term for this. To forgive someone is to show them mercy, not grace.

Grace and mercy are central terms in the New Testament. Grace is used 124 times, and mercy is used 53 times. They are used in the same verse four times, each time in a list,

---

[2] "Evangelical" is not an officially defined term. When I use it, I am referring to denominations and Christians that 1.) emphasize evangelism, 2.) consider the Bible divinely inspired and the only authority for Christians, and 3.) believe in being born again through faith. Usually, "evangelical" is not capitalized because it is a movement, not an organization.

one right after another (1 Tim. 1:2; 2 Tim. 1:2; Tit. 1:4; 2 Jn. 3). Surely they do not mean the same thing!

I encourage you to pause here and consider the last time that you used the word "grace." Ask yourself if you could have used the word "mercy" in its place. We all know the meaning of the word mercy. Surely, even if grace includes mercy, it must mean something more.

And, in fact, this is exactly what we find in the Scriptures.

> To Timothy, my own son in the faith, be grace, mercy and peace from God our Father and King Jesus our Lord. (1 Tim. 1:2)[3]

Here Paul blesses Timothy with grace, mercy, and peace. He would have found alternative words if grace and mercy were synonyms, meaning the same thing.

The writer of Hebrews gives us an excellent contrast between grace and mercy:

> Let us therefore come boldly to the throne of grace, so that we may obtain mercy and grace to help in time of need. (Heb. 4:16)

We know what "mercy" means. It is the forgiveness of sins. However, we see in Hebrews 4:16 that those who come to the "throne of grace" are offered something more than mercy. "Grace" is also offered and, whatever we might consider grace to mean, it must be something that will "help in time of need."

---

[3] I remind the reader that unless otherwise noted, Scripture references are taken from the King James Version, then updated to modern wording and punctuation. I have also chosen "King" as a translation of the Greek *Christos*, which is usually left untranslated (transliterated) as Christ. The reasons for this are given in the notes that begin this book.

Grace in the New Testament

There are four verses I like to use to explain grace because they describe the benefits of grace so well. In fact, I prefer to say that they explain what grace *does* very well, because the favor of God is not inactive. When you are in God's favor, that favor will pursue you with its benefits.

You have already seen the first verse and the first action of grace in Hebrews 4:16: grace will help in time of need. The second is ...

Romans 6:14

> Sin shall not have dominion over you, for you are not under Law but under grace. (Rom 6:14)

Here Paul tells us that sin will not have power over us, something not all of us believe, but something that we should all believe. He also tells us *why* sin won't have power over us. It is because we are not under law, but under grace. God's favor, says Paul, frees us from sin's dominion.

How grace does that bring us to the third verse that explains grace.

Titus 2:11-12

> For the grace of God, that which saves everyone, has appeared, teaching us that denying ungodliness and worldly lusts, we should live righteously, soberly and godly in this present age ... (Tit. 2:11-12)

What happened to the forgiveness of sins? Why is it not mentioned here?

Grace comes to those that have already received mercy because of their belief that Jesus is the King (Christ), the

Son of the Living God. Mercy comes first, by the same means that grace comes, through faith. Mercy means that our sins are forgiven, and grace delivers us from sin's power (Rom. 6:14). The combination is powerful. Mercy from God means that our old sins are forgotten, and Grace means that we can overcome sin in the future.

In fact, grace *teaches* us what overcoming sin looks like. As I said, God's favor is an active favor. It does not sit, waiting for you to come take advantage of it, like that of my friend's dictator uncle. It *appears* and it *teaches*. It is *active*.

It teaches us to "deny ungodliness and worldly lusts." This, combined with our deliverance from the dominion of sin through grace, allows us to follow the teaching of grace and live "righteously, soberly, and godly in this present age."

In the past, right about now is where I asked, "What about me? Why am I not experiencing this amazing deliverance?" The last half of this booklet will address living out a grace-empowered life.

Before we go on to the fourth verse that expands and completes our description of grace, let's look at a couple verses to strengthen what we have already seen.

Ephesians 2:8-9

Most evangelicals know and love Ephesians 2:8-9, but without a proper definition of grace, we miss its power. In fact, we miss the reason that verse 10 should always be included with verses 8-9.

> For by grace are you saved through faith, and that not of yourselves, but as a gift from God, not of works, so that no one may boast. For we are his handiwork, created in King Jesus to do good works, which God has prepared in advance for us to do. (Eph. 2:8-10)

There are many important truths tucked away in this passage, but we are going to have to content ourselves with the surface ones in this short treatise.

We see that it is "by" grace that we are saved, and it is "through" faith. The Greek of this passage makes "of" or "from" grace a better rendering than "by," but the difference in meaning between the three words is insignificant for our purposes. We will content ourselves with looking at "by grace" and "through faith."

The difference between "by" grace and "through" faith is exactly the same difference we see in Paul's description of the creation of everything. In 1 Corinthians 8:6, he tells us that all things are "of" or "out of" the Father and that all things are "through" the Son.[4]

Just as the Father created all things through the Son, so that the source of all things is the Father and the channel for the work was the Son, so the source of salvation in Ephesians 2:8 is grace, and the channel through which we receive grace is faith.

Though Paul is inconsistent in his use of words, he tells us in Romans 5:1-2 in even clearer terms that grace has been channeled to us through faith:

> Therefore, being justified by faith, we have peace with God through our Lord Jesus the King, through whom **we have access by faith to this grace in which we stand**. (Romans 5:1-2a, emphasis mine)

Here Paul uses a different word for the role of faith than he does in Ephesians 2:8, saying that we are justified "by" or

---

[4] The KJV says that all things are "by" the Son, but the translation is wrong, at least in modern English. The Greek word used in 1 Corinthians 8:6 concerning the Son is *dia*, exactly the same word used in Ephesians 2:8 concerning faith. In almost all cases, it is properly translated "through."

"out of" faith rather than through faith. He nonetheless explains in simple terms that faith gives us access to the grace by which we stand.

Faith is a means. It is a means to the forgiveness of sins, which is mercy, and it also provides access to grace, which breaks sin's power over us (Rom. 6:14), helps us in time of need (Heb. 4:16), and teaches us to live godly lives (Tit. 2:11-12).

We have one more passage to explore to firm up the explanation I am giving for grace.

Acts 2:38

> Then Peter said to them, "Repent and be baptized, every one of you, in the name of Jesus the King for the remission of sins, and you shall receive the gift of the Holy Spirit." (Acts 2:38)

Peter doesn't specifically mention faith here because he had just told the Jews that Jesus is the Lord and Messiah King, risen from the dead. Their cry asking what to do was proof enough that they were "cut to the heart" and were believing in fear, realizing that they had crucified God's eternal King and Son of God. The Jews already believed, so Peter moved on to the proper response to the message they believed.

The proper response, said Peter, is to repent and be baptized in the name of Jesus, the Messiah King that he had just announced, and Peter promised them two things in return. We are not used to thinking in these terms, but what he promised them boils down to mercy and grace.[5]

---

[5] I am aware that many (most?) evangelicals do not agree with me that Peter said baptism is for the remission of sins. I have always believed, and find it impossible not to believe, that it is always best to believe Scripture in its plainest sense. I have found this principle makes the Scriptures remarkably consistent

The promises Peter made were that the Jews would receive forgiveness of sins, which we know is mercy, and the gift of the Holy Spirit. We are not used to equating the gift of the Holy Spirit with grace, but think about the overlap between what the Scriptures say about the Holy Spirit and about grace.

We have learned that grace delivers us from the dominion of sin and teaches us to deny ungodliness and worldly lusts and live godly and righteously. Prior to beginning this booklet, if I had asked you how we are delivered from sin and taught to live righteously, you would have said, "by the Holy Spirit," and you would have been correct.

There are many verses explaining that we can only live righteously by the power of the Holy Spirit. Romans 8:13 tells us that we must put to death the deeds of the flesh "by the Spirit." Galatians 5:16 tells us that if we walk in the Spirit we will not fulfill the lusts of the flesh.

I am not saying that the Holy Spirit is grace. The Holy Spirit is the third person of the Trinity, proceeding from the Father, eternal and divine.

I am, however, saying that the Scriptures have a term for the power of the Holy Spirit. That term is "grace."

---

with few difficult verses. If you will search for the words "baptism," "baptized," and "baptize" in the New Testament, you will find that the verses on baptism consistently tell us that the purpose of baptism is the forgiveness of sins and entrance into the King (Christ). The reason that evangelicals fail to see this is because we have replaced baptism with the "sinner's prayer," nowhere found in Scripture. We would understand baptism and its relation to the remission of sins much better were we to return baptism to the place currently occupied by the sinner's prayer, and we would be able to eliminate a whole batch of "difficult verses," namely those like this one and Acts 22:16, which both relate baptism to the forgiveness of sins.

In the very first sentence of this book I said that grace was power. In one sense, this is not true. "Grace" is just a word. All words have meanings, however, and in the Scriptures "grace" is the word that describes the power of the Holy Spirit. We know this because the things grace is described as doing are exactly the same things that the Holy Spirit is described as doing.

Driving this point home brings us to the fourth passage I promised that describes "grace."

Grace: Rounding Out Its Benefits

Here is that fourth verse I promised:

> As everyone has received a gift, serve one another with it as good stewards of the grace of God. (1 Pet. 4:10)

Now this is a fascinating description of grace! The gifts that we receive from the Holy Spirit, as described here, in 1 Corinthians 12, Romans 12, and other places, are gifts of grace. Since we know that it is the Holy Spirit who provides these gifts, one more time we see that "grace" is the word that encompasses the power and work of the Holy Spirit.

This should not surprise us. The Greek word translated "gift" in 1 Peter 4:10 is *charisma*. The Greek word for grace is *charis*. The word the Scripture uses for spiritual gifts is based on the word for grace. This is why some modern translations render *charisma* as "gift of grace."

We know about charismatic gifts like the gift of healing, prophecy, or wisdom (1 Cor. 12:8-10). We are not so familiar with the charismatic gift of deliverance from sin, which is the most important charismatic gift of all!

It may interest you to know that eternal life is called a "charisma," a gift of grace, in Romans 6:23.

It is time to move on to practical applications of this truth. We are about to learn, from the Scripture, how to make use of grace and all the "spiritual gifts" that it imparts, including eternal life.

Living Under Grace

Living under grace is as simple a matter as changing your mind.

This shouldn't surprise us. The Scripture tells us to "be transformed by the renewing of [our] mind" (Rom. 12:1). For most of us, learning to think like a person who has received grace will be a transforming experience indeed!

Far too often we are taught that we are "mere" sinners. Paul rebuked the Corinthians for behaving like mere humans (1 Cor. 3:3). There is nothing "mere" about us.

Peter tells us that God's divine power (grace) has given us *everything* that pertains to life and godliness just because we know Jesus (2 Pet. 1:3). He goes on tell us that we have been given "great and precious promises" so that "through these" we may escape the corruption that is in the world through lust (v. 4). The only way to benefit from a promise is to believe it is true and act on it.

We are not used to thinking of ourselves as having already escaped the corruption that is in the world through lust. We have not been taught, or at least not been sufficiently taught, the great and precious promises of God. Not knowing nor deeply understanding these promises, we go on believing that sin can have power over us, when in fact God has told us through Paul that because we are under grace, sin has no power over us at all (Rom. 6:14).

Soon after telling us we can escape the corruptions of this world (2 Pet. 1:4), Peter speaks as though this escape is a normal part of the Christian life. He warns that those who are entangled in those corruptions a second time will be worse off than before they heard the Gospel (2 Pet. 2:20-21)[6].

It is my experience that only the strongest Christians think of themselves as empowered to overcome the lusts that are in this world. That connection is not coincidental.

The Think System

I've watched *The Music Man* a few times during my life. If you have seen it, you may remember that Harold Hill, the salesman whose corrupt heart would be tamed by the piano teacher, tried to weasel his way out of teaching the band he formed by inventing the "Think System." He cunningly announced, "If you want to play the Minuet in G, you have to *think* the Minuet in G."

As it turned out, the Think System worked. It works even better in the Christian faith.

A friend of mine, in a book called *The Forgotten Gospel*,[7] points out that the very first command in the letters of the apostles is "*Reckon* yourselves to be dead to sin and alive to God in King Jesus" (Rom. 6:11, emphasis mine).

So we find it is not just me, not just *Forgotten Gospel*, but the apostle Paul—and thus our Lord Jesus (1 Cor. 14:37)—who wants us to access grace by the Think System.

> For those that follow the flesh pay attention to the things of the flesh, but those that follow the

---

[6] I know that 2 Peter 2:20-21 is right at the heart of a firestorm over the doctrine of eternal security, or "once saved, always saved." It's not my job to worry about packaged theologies or who holds to them. My job is to teach what the apostles taught and say what the apostles said. It is not a good idea to judge verses based on their relation to any particular denomination's theology or controversy.

[7] Matthew Bryan. [Selmer, TN: Greatest Stories Ever Told™. 2015]. You will find the truths in *Forgotten Gospel* can be a life-changing experience.

> Spirit pay attention to the things of the Spirit. To be fleshly minded is death, but to be spiritually minded is life and peace. (Rom. 8:5-6)

In modern Christianity, we like to think that really walking in the Spirit is impossible for us. Didn't Paul also say "the flesh lusts against the spirit, and the spirit against the flesh ... so that you cannot do the things that you want"? (Gal. 5:17). Didn't Jesus say that apart from him "we can do nothing"? (Jn. 15:5).

Yes, apart from Jesus we can do nothing. Fortunately, *we are not apart from Jesus!*

Romans 8 goes on to explain:

> The fleshly mind is the enemy of God because it is not subject to the law of God, nor can it be. So then, those who are in the flesh cannot please God. (vv. 7-8)

Verses 7 and 8 of Romans 8 could be depressing ... if the chapter ended there.

> But you are not in the flesh, but in the spirit, if the Spirit of God dwells in you. (v. 9)

Paul commanded us to reckon ourselves dead to sin and alive to God in King Jesus, but often we disobey this command because it's hard to see in our lives. It doesn't *appear* to be true, so we reckon it as *not* true.

If we were to be brutally honest with ourselves, we would know this is simple disobedience.

The Example of Moses

Moses gave us an example of exactly that sort of disobedience at the burning bush (Ex. 3:2 – 4:17). Jesus[8] did not react kindly to it.

---

[8] It was Jesus, as the pre-incarnate Word of God, who appeared to Moses in the burning bush. He told the Pharisees, "Before

First, Jesus, as the pre-incarnate Word of God, told Moses he would send him to Pharaoh (3:10). This set off a string of excuses from the man who would become the deliverer, prophet, and first judge of God's holy nation.

- Moses suggested he had no authority to see Pharaoh (3:11). Jesus responded by promising to be with him (3:12).

- Moses objected that the Israelites would not listen (4:1). Jesus gave him two miraculous signs to make them listen (4:2-8), then added a third sign, just in case (4:9).

- Moses objected that he was not eloquent and had difficulty speaking (4:10). Jesus, becoming impatient, asked him who had made his mouth (v. 11). Then he promised to be with Moses' mouth and tell him exactly what to speak (v. 12).

- Finally, Moses straightforwardly asks Jesus to send someone else! (v. 13). That was it. The Scriptures report that Jesus was angry. Frustrated, he gave Moses a replacement speaker, his brother Aaron (14-16), but refused to let Moses out of being the one to perform the signs (v. 17).

It is never a good thing to get God[9] frustrated with you, even if you are Moses. Eventually, this failure to yield to

---

Abraham was, I Am" (Jn. 8:58). Earlier in John's Gospel, we learn that no one has ever seen the Father, not at any time (Jn. 1:18); therefore, we can conclude that all the appearances of God under the Old Covenant were actually "Christophanies," appearances of our pre-incarnate King.

[9] My flip-flop between "Jesus" and "God" in this section and my reference to John 1:18 in the previous footnote are my attempt to interest you in the Trinity as the idea was taught in the apostolic churches and confirmed at the Council of Nicea. You will find no more thorough treatment of the subject than my book, *Decoding*

God would cost him his trip into the Promised Land (Num. 20:7-12).

While overall Moses is an excellent example for us to follow, it is not a good idea to frustrate God the way he did at the burning bush, nor at Meribah, when he was barred from Canaan.

Reckoning vs. Believing

I like the apostle Paul's use of the word "reckon." Reckoning seems much easier to do than believing, though it could be argued that they are exactly the same thing. For me, though, they could not be more different.

Perhaps it is my charismatic experiences in the 1980's, but when the Scriptures ask me to believe, I get nervous. I think, "If I don't believe, then I won't get results, and I am going to be guilty of not bringing something good into the world."

My fear is not unfounded. Mark 11:23-24 tell us about amazing things that we can do if we believe. But if we doubt in our heart? Not so much.

Reckoning is easier, at least for me. God tells me, "Consider it to be so!" I think, okay, I can do that. I'll say it's true. If someone asks me about it, I'll tell them it's true. I'll act like it's true, and I won't allow myself to think anything different.

Reckoning is just thinking. No problem. The fact remains true in my mind, even if I forget to "reckon" here or there. When God tells me, "Regard this as true," somehow I don't feel the same trepidation as when he tells me to "believe." Faith is the evidence of things not seen (Heb. 11:1), so if

---

Nicea, available on Amazon. This series, "Teachings That Must Not Be Lost," will eventually have a booklet on the Trinity as well.

my belief falters, I worry that I have lost my evidence of whatever I am believing for or about.

This is all probably neurotic, but I've asked a few people, and most could relate.

Believing and the Authority of God

Reckoning is simply admitting that what God has told us is true. In one sense, it is no different than believing, but for me it is much different. Reckoning gets my eyes off me and on God, who has said something is true.

God told us, through Paul, that we should reckon ourselves dead to sin and alive to God in King Jesus. When I do so, I am simply acknowledging that what God said is true. My focus is not on me and whether I believe. It is on God, who has told me to think something.

What I am to think is that I am dead to sin. In Romans 6:11 we are told to consider it true, but just a few verses earlier we are told it is true, no matter what we think about it.

> What shall we say then? Shall we continue in sin so that grace may abound? May it never be! How shall we, who are dead to sin, live any longer in it? (Rom. 6:1)

We may not be used to thinking of ourselves in this way, but it is the way God thinks about us and commands us to think about ourselves.

We already think about the apostle Paul this way. He was definitely dead to sin and alive to God in King Jesus. As a matter of fact, he was able to announce, "I am crucified with the King. Nevertheless, I live. Yet not I, but the King lives in me, and the life I live in the flesh I live by faith in the Son of God, who loved me and gave himself for me" (Gal. 2:20).

Paul was doing nothing more than what we are told to do.

Nor did Paul regard himself as different from us. He tells us to imitate him as he imitated our King (1 Cor. 11:1). Surely Paul would not have asked us to do something that we are not equipped to do!

Living by the Life of Jesus

We are not only told to reckon ourselves dead to sin. We are also told to reckon ourselves alive to God in King Jesus.

Paul was doing this, telling us that our King was alive in him, so that all he did was moved and touched both by Jesus and his faith in Jesus.

Repeatedly, he said this is true of us as well.

> But of God are you in King Jesus, who from God has been made to us wisdom, righteousness, holiness, and redemption. (1 Cor. 1:30)

God has made Jesus our wisdom, our righteousness, our holiness, and our redemption. This is true whether you know about it or not. The problem we run into is that most of us don't know it, and so we don't draw on this incredible power inside of us. It is a power with numerous descriptions. It is a power from the Holy Spirit, and it is a power that the Bible calls "grace."

> You are dead, and your life is hidden with the King in God. When the King, who is our life, shall appear, then you will appear with him in glory. (Col. 3:3-4)

Paul knew that he was dead. He knew that his life was hidden away with Jesus in God, and he knew that Jesus was his life.

Now, on the authority of Colossians 3:3-4, we know it, too.

Fighting for Our Thoughts

Now that we reckon and are convinced that we are dead to sin—so that sin does not have power over us—and alive to God in King Jesus, let's talk about how we put that into application.

We have seen that it is the renewing of our mind that transforms us. This begins with reckoning ourselves to be what God has said we are, dead to sin and alive to God in Jesus, but we must go further with this.

> If then, you are risen with the King, seek those things which are above, where the King is sitting at the right hand of God. **Think about** things above, not things on the earth. (Col. 3:1-2, emphasis added)

> We all, with open face, **beholding** as in a mirror the glory of the Lord, are being transformed into that same image from glory to glory, as by the Spirit of the Lord. (2 Cor. 3:18, emphasis added)

> Though our outward man is perishing, yet the inward man is being renewed daily ... **while we look**, not at the things which are seen ... but at the things which are not seen ... (2 Cor. 4:16, 18a, emphasis added)

Instructions like these are throughout the teaching of the apostles. The writer of Hebrews, for example, tells us to "look to Jesus, the Author and Completer of our faith" (Heb. 12:1). Paul tells us that the enemies of the cross "think about earthly things" (Col. 3:19).

We find grace, that power that transforms us into the image of God, when we set our minds on spiritual and heavenly things purposely and on an ongoing basis.

We often say, "He is so heavenly minded that he is of no earthly good." What the Scriptures tell us, however, is that if we don't learn to be heavenly minded—to think about spiritual things—we will fail to be of earthly good.

I suppose this is the reason that in over thirty years as a Christian, I have rarely found a person that is too heavenly minded to be of earthly good, but I have found thousands who are too earthly minded to be of any heavenly good.

This principle is so important that Paul says he was given spiritual weapons, mighty through God, so that he could throw down "imaginations" and every high thing that exalts itself against the knowledge of God. His warfare was all about "bringing every thought into captivity to the obedience of the King" (2 Cor. 10:4-5).

Above all, then, if we want to live in the power provided to us by the grace of God, we have to learn to think differently. We have to renew our minds and thus be transformed. We have to set our minds on things above, look to Jesus, pay attention to unseen, eternal things, and bring every thought into captivity to the obedience of the King.

Fighting the Good Fight

Paul told Timothy, "I have fought the good fight, I have finished the course, I have kept the faith" (2 Tim. 4:7).

It is only after we have renewed our mind, putting off the old man and putting on the new man, King Jesus in us, that we can even begin to fight the good fight. Jesus told us that apart from him we can do nothing. That was not so that we could yield to sin, weakness, and an ineffective, powerless life. He told us that so we would not be apart from him. He tells us repeatedly in John 15, "Remain in me."

Don't misunderstand this command.

Typically, we think, "Oh, no! I stopped thinking about Jesus and about spiritual things for the last twenty minutes.

I have not remained in him. I have lost my power. I am separate from him."

This kind of thinking is destructive, and it doesn't make any sense. It is so common, however, that almost all of us fall into it anyway.

What illustration did Jesus use when he talked about remaining in him? He was describing himself as a vine and us as the branches of that vine.

Does a branch detach from a vine with a passing thought? Or lack of a thought? Do branches suddenly detach themselves, then reconnect themselves?

Is such a bizarre idea what Jesus wanted to illustrate in John 15?

Of course it wasn't. Branches are not detached over and over. If they are detached, they die. Then the workers collect those dead branches and burn them in the fire (Jn. 15:6).

Hudson Taylor spent a whole book explaining this concept. The book is called *Hudson Taylor's Spiritual Secret*. In it, Taylor describes sleeping in a house in China on a very dark night. When he awoke, he couldn't remember where he was.

He used that as an illustration of a "secret" he had not known, nor did most Christians understand. Even though Taylor did not know where he was, and even though he could not see the house, he was still in the house. It didn't matter whether he believed it. The only thing that mattered is that it was true.

Just as Hudson was in the house whether he believed it or not and whether he knew it or not, so he was in King Jesus whether he felt it, believed it, or knew it at that particular moment.

We don't disconnect from the vine because our mind wandered.

If we have confessed that Jesus is Lord, and we have believed in our heart that God raised him from the dead, then according to the Word of God, speaking through Paul in Romans, we are saved (10:9-10). If we are saved, then we are in him. If we are saved, then we have been saved by grace because that is the only way anyone is saved. If we have grace, then sin does not have power over us.

This is true whether we know it or not, whether we understand it or not, and certainly whether we've forgotten about it for a short time or not.

Because that is true, we can engage in the lifelong fight, the lifelong race, that Paul engaged in. Because Paul is not different from us, and because it is the same King Jesus living in us that lived in Paul, then we, too, can obtain a crown laid up for us on the last day, just like Paul did.

That fight, though, is not an easy one.

The Example of Paul

Paul felt that he had to "discipline his body and bring it into subjection" in order not to be "disapproved" after having preached to others (1 Cor. 9:27). He lost everything for Jesus, and considered it to be "manure" (Php. 3:8), leaving it behind to obtain the King and his righteousness, the righteousness which comes through faith in Jesus, is given by God, and rests on faith. All of this, Paul said, was to know him, his power, and even "the fellowship of his sufferings," for the purpose of arriving at the resurrection of the dead (Php. 3:7-11).

He continues in terms fitting for an Olympic athlete in training. He "races after" the King so that he can "seize" whatever it is that King Jesus has "seized him for." He hasn't seized it yet, so he is focused on one thing and one thing only. He forgets everything in the past, and he "stretches out" for the tape at the end of the race. He "races" for the upward call of God in King Jesus (vv. 12-14).

Finally, he ends by telling us that if we are mature in the King, we should think the same way (v. 15).

Clearly, Paul was not laying down on the job. He was going after it at any cost, and he wanted us to do the same. The battle is in the mind, but he is not letting anything get in the way of that battle. He wants a reward at the end, to arrive at the resurrection of the dead, "seizing" whatever Jesus has seized him for, and he is not resting as though he already had it.

The Example of Peter

We have already looked at 2 Peter 1:3-4. There, Peter tells us that God's divine power (grace) has given us everything that pertains to life and godliness. We are lacking absolutely nothing when it comes to life and when it comes to godliness. This is because we have been both trained by grace in how to live godly (Tit. 2:11-12) and empowered by grace to do so (Rom. 6:14).

The source of all this, Peter says, is "the knowledge of him."

Through him, we also have "great and precious promises," and through these we "have escaped"—not "will escape," but "have escaped"—the corruption that is in the world through lust.

Yet despite these great and precious promises, despite the training and empowering of grace, we have something to do.

Perhaps it is better said, *because of* the divine power, which finds its source in knowing him, we have something to do.

Before, when we were slaves to sin, in bondage to the powers and principalities of this world and dead because of our sins (Eph. 2:1-3), we were powerless to do anything good (Rom. 7:18). Now, being no longer powerless, Peter gives us a series of instructions.

We need to add to our faith. Faith gave us access to grace, which we have seen is the divine power that gives us everything that concerns life and godliness. So, with that divine power, he tells us to add to our faith.

It is a beautiful progression of which Peter speaks (2 Pet. 1:5-7).

To faith, we add virtue. All of us come to Jesus with a general idea of what is virtuous. We have a "law" in our conscience (Rom. 2:14-15), and Peter tells us that now that we are empowered we should begin walking in that virtue.

But our earthly, carnal knowledge of virtue is not enough. So to virtue we add knowledge; not the knowledge we were born with in our consciences, but that which comes from God, from the Scriptures (2 Tim. 3:16-17), from our brothers and sisters in the church (Heb. 3:12; 10:24-25). We devote ourselves to the teaching of the apostles and to the commands of Jesus, and we learn the will of the Father.

To knowledge, we add self-control because despite the empowering of God, these things don't just happen. Paul disciplined his body daily (1 Cor. 9:27), and we must do the same.

To self-control, we add perseverance. To control yourself one day is one thing, but to "not grow weary in doing good" is another (Gal. 6:9).

To perseverance, we add godliness. Here is the beginning of the real righteousness of God for which Paul strove. Here our study, our self-control, and our perseverance pay off as we become more than diligent disciples. Our work begins to get inside us, transforming us. The writer of Hebrews calls it maturity, and he describes the mature as those who "through practice have their senses exercised to discern good and evil" (5:14).

To godliness, we add brotherly love (Gr. *philadelphia*). We are commanded from the beginning to love one another, but it is only as the righteousness of God, that which rests on faith and comes from perseverance in knowledge and self-control, is formed in us that we love with a love that comes from God.

That brotherly love is what will take us to the last and final goal: God's love (Gr. *agape*[10]). God is love, and as his righteousness is formed in us, it will move toward one thing: love.

This happens by renewing our mind, as we saw earlier, but the renewing of our mind, as we are seeing from Paul and Peter, is no small thing. Even in the original mention of renewing our mind, Paul ties it to presenting our body as a living sacrifice, something he calls our "reasonable worship" (Rom. 12:1).

We have to set our minds on things above. This will stop our minds from focusing on the things of the flesh. Renewing our minds will transform us, but we will not find it easy. If Paul had to make a habit of discipline and subjecting his body (1 Cor. 9:27), then we will need to do so as well. Peter says we will need to "make every effort" (2 Pet. 1:10). Jesus certainly made every effort for us! (Heb. 12:2-3; 1 Pet. 1:18-19).

---

[10] *Agape* is an awesome word. It's hard to find a meaning for it in classical Greek, but Jesus (or the apostles, since Jesus actually spoke Aramaic, not Greek) adapted the word to describe the kind of love that only God can produce. That love is the proof that we are Jesus' disciples (Jn. 13:34-35).

The rewards of progress in the faith are phenomenal. Not only will we find ourselves having escaped the corruption that is in the world through lust, but if we are diligent in the things Peter spoke of, we will never stumble, never be barren, never be unfruitful, and gain an "abundant entrance" into the everlasting kingdom of our Lord and Savior, Jesus the King (2 Pet. 1:8-11).

This is the grace of God as taught by the Scriptures. There seems to be other versions of grace being taught by evangelicals today. At least one of those versions is specifically warned against in Scripture.

Changing the Grace of God

> Certain men have slipped in secretly ... ungodly men, changing the grace of God into wantonness and denying the only Lord God and our Lord Jesus the King. (Jude 4)

The lead-in to this verse is interesting. Jude was going to write a general letter talking about our "common salvation," but he couldn't. Instead, he found it "necessary" to exhort them to "contend earnestly for the faith once delivered to the saints" (v. 3).

Why? Because "certain men have slipped in secretly ... changing the grace of God."

Those men were changing the grace of God into an excuse for lust. The New International Version translates that phrase as "into a license for immorality."

In my own experience, and I suspect in yours as well, we are perilously close to doing this in evangelical churches as well. It is not an exception, but common, for an exhortation to righteousness to be met or followed with "Let's remember that we are saved by grace." This is said by those who make grace a synonym for mercy, but most evangelicals belong to that group. So they are carefully taking the sting away from exhortations to live righteously by pointing out that we are already forgiven *even if we ignore the exhortation.*

They expect exhortations to righteousness to be ignored or impossible to receive because they have not been told about, nor do they understand, most of the benefits of living in God's favor.

Worse is when reproof for sin is met by using grace to parry the reproof.

Jesus tells us that if a brother sins against us, we should rebuke him (Jn. 17:3). Two of the four uses that Paul lists for the Scriptures are reproof and correction. One of the other two is "instruction in righteousness" (2 Tim. 3:16). The only purpose he gives for the Scriptures in that passage is "that the man of God may be thoroughly equipped for every good work" (v. 17).

Grace is the means by which we can act on reproof, rebuke, correction, and instruction in righteousness. Grace empowers us to be able to be thoroughly equipped for every good work, delivering us from the law of sin and death, which left us crying out, "Who shall rescue me from this body of death!" (Rom. 7:18; 8:2).

When we tell someone who reproves us for sin to remember that we are saved by grace, we are changing grace into something that it is not. In fact, we are changing grace into an excuse for sin, something that false teachers did in the first century. Jude had some awful things to say about them, even calling them "blights on your love feasts" (v. 12).

Grace should drive us toward righteousness and good works, not give us an excuse to turn away from them.

True Grace vs. False Grace

Peter said that his first letter was written to exhort and testify "that this is the true grace of God in which you stand" (1 Pet. 5:12). When someone exhorts and testifies about a true grace of God, this presupposes that there is a false one.

Peter would go on to write a second letter with a chapter remarkably similar to the letter of Jude (2 Peter 2). He knew there was a false grace of God, a teaching that grace was an excuse for sin. He used much the same words as Jude:

> They allure through the lusts of the flesh, [through] wantonness, those truly escaped from those who live in error. While they promise them freedom, they themselves are the slaves of corruption. For of whom a man is overcome, of him he is he enslaved. (2 Pet. 2:18-19)

We are warned to beware of false grace and to "contend earnestly" for the true grace of God, the faith once delivered to the saints.

Faith and Works

No doctrine is as important to evangelicals as "salvation by faith alone," or salvation "apart from works."

The Scriptures definitely teach us that salvation is apart from works, saying, "By grace are you having been saved by faith, and that [salvation] not of yourselves, it is the gift of God, not of works, lest anyone should boast" (Eph. 2:8-9). We looked at this passage earlier.

Elsewhere, Paul directly contrasts grace and works:

> And if by grace, then it is no longer by works. Otherwise grace is no longer grace. But if of works, then it is no longer by grace, otherwise work is no longer work. (Rom. 11:6)

There is no starker contrast than this. The two, at least as a source of salvation (or, in context, election), are incompatible.

Yet we have learned in this little treatise that grace is all about producing works. Paul ties it right in with Ephesians 2:8-9, which I have argued should never be quoted without verse 10: "For we are his workmanship, created in King Jesus for good works, which God has prepared in advance for us to do."

Paul ties good works in with grace in Titus 2, following his description of the teaching of grace in verses 11-12 with this description of the purpose of Jesus' death: "... who gave himself for us that he might redeem us from all iniquity and purify for himself his own special people, zealous for good works" (v. 14).

What is all this? How can grace be given as completely incompatible with works so that the two cannot be mixed as the source of salvation without destroying the meaning of one or the other, then grace be said to be the source of works that apparently admit us into the kingdom of God and give us eternal life? (2 Pet. 1:10-11; Gal 6:8-9).

Evangelicals have assumed that when Paul talks about justification in Romans 3, he is talking about the full range of salvation, from our experience of being baptized, being born again, and entering a new life in King Jesus all the way to the judgment, where we will be automatically admitted to the eternal kingdom, also completely apart from works.

A quick run through the passages on the judgment will make it clear that this is not accurate. Jesus describes the judgment in Matthew 25:31-46, and there the difference between the sheep and the goats is based solely on their deeds. The sheep receive everlasting life for their good deeds, and the goats enter the everlasting fire for their lack of good deeds.

In John 5:29, Jesus said again that the difference between those who go to a resurrection of condemnation and those who go to a resurrection of life is a matter of who did evil and who did good.

As though he wanted to make sure we knew this was true of Christians as well as non-Christians, Paul says, "We shall all stand before the judgment seat of the King, to receive the deeds done in the body, whether good or bad" (2 Cor. 5:10).

Peter, too, wanted to make sure we know this includes Christians: "If you address as Father the one who impartially judges according to each person's work, then conduct yourself throughout the time of your sojourning here in fear" (1 Pet. 1:17).

Jesus did not limit his admonitions about the judgment to his time on earth. In Revelation 2 and 3, he wrote letters to the churches, continuously mentioning their works, ignoring their faith, and making promises to those who overcome and threats to those who did not. In fact, one of the most frightening verses directed at Christians in the entire Bible is in the letter to Sardis at the start of Revelation 3. "You have a few names even in Sardis," Jesus says, "who have not defiled their garments."

Wow. Just a few names? What will happen to them?

"They will walk with me in white, for they are worthy" (Rev. 3:4).

Jesus goes on. "He that overcomes will be clothed in white garments, and I will not blot his name out of the Book of Life, but I will confess his name before my Father and before his messengers" (v. 5).[11] Obviously, he is threatening to blot the name of those who do not overcome out of the Book of Life, something that would apply to the majority of the Christians in Sardis!

Born Again Through Faith and the Judgment by Works

Paul does teach that we are "justified" by faith. It is coming out more and more today, even among evangelicals, that "justified" refers to right standing with God in the sense of being a good and accepted member of God's kingdom, his

---

[11] *Angellos* is another word that is not translated, but transliterated, in our Bibles. We simply write out the Greek letters in English as "angel." *Angellos* has a meaning. It is "messenger," and it is used several times of earthly messengers in the New Testament as well (Matt. 11:10; Luke 9:52). You don't know that because our Bibles only translate *angellos* as messenger when it refers to human messengers, making a distinction between earthly and heavenly messengers that Jesus and the apostles did not make.

covenant community.[12] It means having all the rights of those in covenant with God.

These rights can be summed in the word "grace" that we have been looking at. "Justified" means that we are in the favor of God, and we have seen that God's favor is active, teaching us a new way of life and empowering us to live it.

We have also seen that the apostles expect us to diligently obey the teaching of grace and to walk in the power it brings. Peter even tells us that if we are entangled in the corruptions of the world again, then we are worse off than before we began. It would have been better for us "never to have known the way of righteousness" than to turn away from "the holy commandment" delivered to us (2 Pet. 2:20-21).

Jude warns us of false teachers who would turn the grace of God into a license for immorality (v.4). The apostle John warns us not to be deceived into believing the people who tell us that we can have the righteousness of Jesus without actually living righteously.

> Little children, don't let anyone deceive you. **The one that is doing righteousness is righteous just as he is righteous.** The one that goes on committing sin is of the devil. (1 Jn. 3:7, emphasis mine)

It would be impossible for John to be much clearer, wouldn't it? He gives it a whirl a chapter earlier, though.

> This is how we know that we are knowing him, if we are keeping his commandments. The one that says, "I am knowing him," but is not keeping his commandments is being a liar, and the truth is not in him. (1 Jn. 2:3-4)

---

[12] N.T. Wright's *What St. Paul Really Said* is a great example of such books.

I apologize for the awkwardness of the wording, but the Greek present tense in John is very important. Our English tenses do not convey continual, ongoing action, but the Greek present tense does. Every Greek class you attend or Greek lesson book you read will tell you that the present tense should be translated "is knowing" or "is keeping" to convey the continuous or repeated action.

First John can be a frightening book without knowing this! John is never talking about individual sins or a single disobedient act. The righteous are marked by an ongoing obedience to Jesus' commands, made possible by grace, and the children of the devil are marked by an ongoing obedience to their own ways, ignoring Jesus' commands.

John knows we all sin. He says that the person who says they are without sin is a liar (1 Jn. 1:8). He tells us that if we do sin, Jesus is our *parakletos*, our comforter and advocate with the Father (1 Jn. 2:1). It is the same word used of the Holy Spirit in John 14:26.

By grace, through faith, we are brought into this life. In this life, we can expect to sin and be forgiven (mercy), but we must also expect to overcome sin on an ongoing basis (grace), growing in our righteousness before God (2 Pet. 1:8).

This puts us in a good position for the judgment, which the Scripture repeatedly says is by works, never mentioning faith.

This is why James seems to absolutely contradict Paul, saying that we are justified by works and not by faith only (2:24). This is not a contradiction, of course. James is covering the whole sweep of the Christian life, from being born again through the judgment. This does require both faith, which obtains grace for us, and works, which are obtained by grace. Paul, however, in Romans 3:28, is speaking only of our deliverance from slavery to sin, which is accomplished solely by the grace brought to us through faith.

The Judgment

Fortunately, we can expect to reach the judgment with a clean record. If we have walked in the light, then Jesus' blood has been continually cleansing us from sin (1 Jn. 1:7). If we have been confessing our known sins, then we can expect that they have been forgiven (1 Jn. 1:9). God is a kind and merciful God, whose mercies are new every morning (Lam. 3:22). He does not just pardon, he *abundantly* pardons (Isa. 55:7).

This is why Jude ends his rant against those who change the grace of God into a license for immorality by saying, "Now to him who is able to keep you from falling, and to present you faultless before the presence of his glory with exceptional joy, to the only wise God our Savior, be glory and majesty, dominion and power, both now and forever" (vv. 24-25).

We are not saved by works. We enter into the grace of God, which the Scripture says saves all men (Tit. 2:11), through faith and apart from works (Eph. 2:8-9).

That grace breaks sin's power over us, allowing us to put to death the deeds of the body by the power of the Spirit (Rom. 8:12-13). Thus, along with the daily cleansing of Jesus' blood (1 Jn. 1:7), we arrive at the throne of God faultless with exceeding joy (Jude 23).

There we will be judged by our works, not by our faith, in an impartial judgment that will not treat Christians any differently than non-Christians (1 Pet. 1:17; cf. Eph. 5:5-8; 1 Cor. 10:1-12; Rom. 2:5-8; 11:19-22).

This last teaching about justification by faith and a judgment by works is probably new if you are an evangelical, but really, we are the only ones not in the know. Not only is the New Testament 100% consistent on the subject, but so is the teaching of the church for almost 1500 years. If Jesus or the apostles taught that we could bypass the judgment by our faith, then they were terrible communicators because no one figured that out until the sixteenth century!

We will look deeper into this in the booklet on faith and works in this "Teachings that Must Not Be Lost" series.

Summing Up Grace

Grace means favor. A friend of mine suggested that this is the equivalent of "generosity," a word that might carry even more meaning for us than favor, especially coming from God.

We have seen that God's favor, or generosity, is active, both breaking the power of sin and teaching us to how to live godly lives in this present age. However, we have also seen that we have to appropriate the power that comes from God's grace. In fact, if we want to enter the everlasting Kingdom of God, we must diligently appropriate grace to put to death the deeds of the body (Rom. 8:12-13) by renewing our mind (Rom. 12:1-2), bringing our body under subjection (1 Cor. 9:27), and continually adding to our faith (2 Pet. 1:3-11) without growing weary in doing good (Gal. 6:7-9).

We have learned to beware of those who would change the grace of God into wantonness, making it a license for immorality (Jude 4). We must stand in the true grace of God (1 Pet. 5:10-12), to which we have access by faith (Rom. 5:2).

Above all, we have learned to regard what God has said about us as true. We are dead to sin and alive to God in King Jesus (Rom. 6:11; cf. v. 3; Col. 3:1-4).

We have learned that all of this, even the subjection of our body, is accomplished by constantly turning our eyes toward Jesus (Heb. 12:2), setting our mind on the Spirit (Rom. 8:5-8), and paying attention to spiritual, unseen things, which are eternal (2 Cor. 3:19; 4:18).

We have also learned that while those walking in the grace of God are marked by their obedience to God's commands and their righteous lives (1 Jn. 2:3-4; 3:7-8), there is no one that does not sin (1 Jn. 1:8). When we do sin, we have a helper/comforter/advocate with the Father, King Jesus the righteous one (1 Jn. 2:1). In addition, God is already faithful and just to forgive our sins and cleanse us from all unrighteousness when we confess our sins and walk in the light (1 Jn. 1:7,9).

This is grace, and this is the life of grace. It is in this "true grace of God" that we have joy unspeakable and full of glory (1 Pet. 1:8).

About the Author

Paul Pavao is a teacher and a writer. He has been a leading teacher at Rose Creek Village, a Christian community of around two hundred people, for over ten years. He now leads a house church in Memphis.

Paul is the author of *Decoding Nicea*, the thoroughly researched story of the Council of Nicea, and *The Apostles' Gospel*, a comparison of the apostolic preaching in the book of Acts with the gospel preached by evangelicals today. Paul is also the webmaster of Christian-history.org, a web site on the early churches, the Council of Nicea, and the Reformation, and paulfpavao.com, a web site and blog containing all his other Christian writings.

Paul lives in Memphis, TN with his wife and two youngest children.

www.ingramcontent.com/pod-product-compliance
Lightning Source LLC
Chambersburg PA
CBHW051959290426
44110CB00015B/2303